Soccer Drills

Improve Your Team's Possession and Passing Skills through Top Class Drills

Chest Dugger

Table Of Contents

About The Author

Disclaimer

Introduction

Teamwork – The Importance of Possession and Passing

The Mentality of the Team – Incorporating the 'Star' Player

Individual Passing Drills

Team Passing Drills

Individual Possession Drills

Team Possession Drills

Conclusion

About The Author

Chest Dugger is a soccer fan, former professional and coach, looking to share his knowledge. Enjoy this book and several others that he has written.

Disclaimer

Copyright © 2018

All Rights Reserved

No part of this eBook can be transmitted or reproduced in any form including print, electronic, photocopying, scanning, mechanical, or recording without prior written permission from the author.

While the author has taken the utmost effort to ensure the accuracy of the written content, all readers are advised to follow information mentioned herein at their own risk. The author cannot be held responsible for any personal or commercial damage caused by information. All readers are encouraged to seek professional advice when needed.

Introduction

Soccer is the world's most popular sport. In the Summer of 2018 the next World Cup Finals take place in Russia, with some of the best (and, perhaps, luckiest) teams in the world participating. The competition will see teams divided into mini leagues, based on their world rankings and a draw. The top two teams from each group go forward to the knock out stages.

The best two will compete in the final. There is a more than reasonable bet that existing champions Germany will once again lift the trophy, although Brazil, Argentina, Spain and France will all fancy their chances. The Belgians have the team of a life time, and could triumph, while the likes of Saudi Arabia and Panama should make the most of their time in Eastern Europe – it will probably be short lived. As for Russia itself, the lowest ranked side in the competition, well, who knows? Home advantage can count for a lot.

This short focus on the World Cup is of great relevance to the book that follows. Consider the team below:

Goalkeepers: Jan Oblak, stalwart of the Spanish giants Athletico Madrid – a team whose recent success in challenging the established giants of La Liga, Real Madrid and Barcelona, has been built on gritty, defiant defending; Gianluigi Buffon, legendary player between the posts.

Defenders: David Alaba, kingpin of Bayern Munich; Antonio Valencia, rampaging wing back of Manchester United and Virgil van Dijk, the most highly rated defender in England's Premier League, just transferred for a record (for a defender) fee approaching $100 million, Giorgio Chiellini, tough, no nonsense centre back with more than a touch of skill.

Midfielders: Christian Pulisic, Borussio Dortmand's well regarded midfielder; Arjen Robben, the Bayern Munich and former Chelsea wizard of the wing; Daniele De Rossi, a central defensive midfielder who would walk into any team in the world.

Attackers: Alexis Sanchez, at the time of writing, European powerhouse Arsenal's outstanding player; Gareth Bale, the Real Madrid attacking maestro; Pierre Emerick Aubameyang, one of the most promising strikers on the planet.

Those of you with good football knowledge will spot that these great players, along with many more, are some of the giants of the game who will not feature in the World Cup Finals, other than perhaps in the commentary box, pundit's chair or newspaper columns of June 2018.

How can this be? How can such individuals not represent their countries on the biggest stage of all? The answer, as we know, is that soccer is a team game, where the collective talents of the players outweigh the individual skills of the maestro. The great sides do, naturally, incorporate such talents within their squad, but it is so often the case that a team that works together and combines well outperforms a side made up of more talented individuals who are less effective team players.

And the secret to success is possession of the football. Passing, and the possession this helps to retain, really are two of the most important parts of team play for a soccer team. This book will look at a number of ways both coaches and players can improve such aspects of their own side's performance.

Teamwork – The Importance of Possession and Passing

There is a saying in soccer, a rather obvious one, that goes something like 'You can't score if you don't have the ball… and the opposition won't put the ball in the net if you do.' The clever clogs of the planet quickly point out 'own goals', but we get the idea. Certainly, some teams like to play on the break, utilising quick passing and speed to catch the opposition during transition (the point at which the ball is lost or regained). We will look at teams that like to play on the break later in the chapter, but as a general rule, the more your side has the ball, the more likely it is to score and the less likely it is to concede.

In general terms, it is seen that there are three phases in soccer. Offence, or attack, when your side has the ball; defence, when your team does not have the ball, and transition, the stage between the two.

It therefore makes sense that a team will wish to be in attack more than defence, in other words have the ball in their possession more than leave it with the opposition.

There are five elements to retaining possession, and we will look at each one in turn. These stages, in no particular order, are receiving the ball and controlling it; dribbling, passing, communication and movement off the ball.

Receiving the Ball/Control

The ball can be received by either foot on the ground, off the ground using the feet up to around knee height; on the thigh; on the chest and with the head. There are then three positions through which the player might receive the ball, these being, head on with back to goal; on the half turn; and a pass on which to run.

Let us look at each of these in a little more detail.

Feet on the ground: The best players should be comfortable receiving the ball with either foot. Practice on the weaker foot, even as simple as hitting the ball against a wall and controlling it fifty times a day will soon make the less comfortable foot more than simply something for standing on. The foot should 'cushion' the ball as it comes in by slightly relaxing it, 'giving' a little to the ball. This means that the ball will not bounce away, and nor will it become stuck under the foot. Weight should be over the ball, and as much body should be behind the ball as possible, to prevent an opponent from nicking it away. Controlling a pass with feet on the ground is the easiest method and this is why most coaches encouraging passing 'on the deck'. The ball is usually controlled with the inside of the foot, but by using the outside of the foot it is possible to turn quickly, beating your marker. Controlling with the toes, a difficult skill, will slightly lift the ball and might draw a foul from a tight marker, as they lunge in for the ball, thinking it has been miss-controlled.

Feet off the ground: Here, it is important for the receiver to get into position as soon as possible. They should have a check to see what kind of pressure the defence is able to put on them, and bend the knee of the receiving foot to make the leg into a triangle. Control is with the instep. If pressure is on, then usually a player will control with their first touch and lay off a pass with their second. Team mates can anticipate this, getting into position if they sense that an early pass is likely.

The kind of lifted pass that requires control in this way can be used to put some swerve on the ball allowing it to be played round an opponent, and is also one which often draws a defender forward, and can create a little space behind this player.

Thigh Control: A more difficult skill again. The thigh of the receiving leg comes slightly forward and the knee bends to create a triangle. This should not be too steeply angled, as the maximum area possible of the thigh should be exposed. Since balance is harder to maintain here, as it is likely that the receiving leg is off the ground, and weight is over it, the arms need to be out for balance. These also make it harder for a defender to get around and make a tackle.

Chest Control: The receiver should check for challenges likely to come in, spread their arms to make as big an area as possible and ensure that their body continues to protect the ball as it is received. More experienced players will close their arms at the last minute to make the ball drop to their feet more quickly, and a good skill to practise is twisting the body on receipt to direct the ball to a team mate. This 'chest pass' to an on-running team mate can really create space and lead to a driving run and attack, especially around the penalty area where space might be tight and a pass along the ground hard to orchestrate.

Head: There are many types of headers, but as we are looking at retaining possession here, rather than attempting a goal or clearing the ball, we will focus on two types – the flick on and the cushioned header. The flick on is designed to put the ball into the space behind the defence for an attacker to run on to. To be successful there has to be a good understanding between the striker and his team mate. Both need to anticipate the flick, to allow for the run to be made with good timing. Usually, the player heading the ball will be marked by the last defender, and if the run off the ball is not timed well, the player will fall offside. There is little force behind the flick on, the ball just (to state the obvious) flicked by the attacker's head. The pace of the ball takes it into the space behind the defence. The flick on can be effective, but is not a good way to retain possession. Firstly, it is likely the passer will be under pressure and therefore controlling the flick is difficult; secondly, often a defending team will drop a defender back in anticipation of the move. The cushioned header is a controlled, directed header to a close by team mate, often the goalkeeper. Here, the body is held firmly and the head directs the ball to the team mate, relaxing slightly on contact with the ball to take the pace off the pass.

Next, we will consider the three ways in which possession is maintained with the receipt of the pass.

Half Turn: This is the most effective way to receive a pass and retain possession. Here, the shoulder is directed towards the passer, and the body twists to receive the ball at between 30 and 45 degrees. The body is slightly crouched, with knees loose and slightly bent, to allow for a strong, low centre of gravity, plus movement in all directions. The ball can then be received on the instep to allow for a return pass, or to move the ball forwards (if under no pressure) or towards the player's own goal (if some pressure is felt); on the outside of the boot to allow for a spin to turn into space or beat a defender, or on the toes to lift the ball and buy a little time, or encourage a tackle to earn a free kick. Watch players at the highest level, and their receipt of the ball will often be on the half turn. The first touch here is very important, as less of the body is protecting the ball, and if the touch is poor, possession is likely to be lost. Scouts for professional clubs and those teaching children for the highest levels will usually look for the player's first touch – if this is missing, it is unlikely that the player will be selected for trials at a more advanced level.

Back to goal: The arms are outstretched for balance and protection. The body shields the ball, with the back facing the opponents goal. Communication is important, where team mates tell the receiver whether they have time to turn, are under closing pressure, or need a one or two touch lay off. Often with this kind of receipt, the player will lay the ball back the way they are facing, that is, towards their own goal, to a team mate in more space, then make a move into space themselves. 'Back to Goal' can be a slightly misleading term, as this way of receiving the ball can also be from a lateral pass, where the player has his or her back to the touchline, although this will usually only be in and around the attacking penalty area.

Running on to the ball: This is an attacking pass into space for a player to dribble, pass or cross. A pass that allows for the running on to the ball injects pace into an attack, while the side continues to retain possession.

Dribbling

Running with the ball into space, or beating an opponent with the ball under tight control. Dribbling is exciting to watch, commits defenders and can create space for the team in possession. The best players show patience and game awareness when dribbling. They will make the judgement when to turn back, perhaps to lay a pass off to a team mate, or wait for a player to run past them to create either space for themselves (if their defender follows the run) or to play a simple pass into space for this attacker.

Weaker players, with less understanding of the game, will hold on to the ball for too long, missing the chance to pass to a player in a better position, or trying to beat one defender too many and losing possession.

Communication

All aspects of soccer require good communication. This is especially true if the aim is to maintain possession. Communication gives more information to team mates than that which they can see, sense or hear. It also gives an insight into what the communicator is about to do. Go to watch a professional match and sit close to the pitch, and the noise from the players is non-stop, they are communicating with each other continuously. This is a good objective for any level or age of team.

Because players in possession are could be under pressure, or playing at great speed, communication needs to be simple and direct. Calls such as 'Turn' or 'Line' are more effective than multi word phrases – this friendlier type of communication can be given during a break in play!

Passing

To a large extent, we have covered the importance of passing to keep possession in the section on control. However, a side losing possession can often be traced back to a poor pass – a lifted pass when one on the ground would have been better might lead to the recipient finding it tougher to control, and thus being put under more pressure by an opponent – their subsequent pass might therefore lack accuracy, or be rushed, leading to a transfer of possession.

Movement off the ball

Players who move well off the ball make it easier for the team to keep possession. These are the selfless players, prepared to work for the good of the team, to get themselves in a position for a pass that perhaps never comes. But their runs create space. That space comes either to themselves, because they have run into it and given the player in possession an easy option for a pass. Or that space can be created for a team mate, because they draw away a defender. A key reason why teams that play well together are more successful than one of talented individuals is that willingness to make life easier for team mates. Players simply improve when they have time.

Playing on the Break

We have promoted the value and importance of keeping possession, and continue to support this as the best way for success. Nevertheless, some teams do set up to play on the break. This could be because they recognise that they are weaker than the opposition, and wish to keep their defensive structure for most of the time, before hitting quickly at the transition point. It could also be that their players fit this system well. Whichever, it is very hard to play on the break without good running off the ball and speed.

The key to playing on the break is to be very organised. Firstly, the defensive and midfield structures need to be solid, to cause the opposition to lose possession and allow for the transition phase.

Secondly, players need to recognise when possession is about to be lost, and know their responsibilities at this transition point.

Passing options need to be quickly created to exploit the disorganisation in the side that has just lost the ball, and the ball needs to be moved quickly, with accurate passing into space and good dribbling skills. Finally, not every break will result in a shot on goal, which means that transition is likely to change again. Therefore, the side hitting on the break need to also retain their own defensive structure in anticipation of losing possession again.

The point about ending in a shot is important; one of the key elements of playing on the break is that there should be a goal attempt at the end. Even if it does not result in a score, the shot gives the attacking team time to reorganise (from the resulting goal kick, for example) after their play.

The Mentality of the Team – Incorporating the 'Star' Player

The star player. So often a cause of mixed feelings among fans, coaches and fellow team mates. Of course, we must be wary of generalisations. There are many 'special ones' from the highest level who are also excellent team players. Lionel Messi is, apparently, a great bloke who gives his all for his team mates. Steven Gerrard, the former Liverpool and England central midfield maestro was brilliant with the younger members of the squad.

Others, though, recognise their brilliance and can appear intolerant of the lesser abilities of their colleagues. However, integrating the star maverick is the job of the coach. Getting such a player to buy into the methods of the team can lead to that player offering an enormous amount to the success of the side.

Let us consider the typical characteristics of the star maverick.

- Often, players such as these find it hard to accept the team goals unless they are made explicit.
- They challenge expected practices and procedures.
- They are often very creative, both in their play and also in their understanding of the flow of the game.

- Mavericks can lack their own skills in putting across their points of view or in asking their questions. This can see them labelled as arrogant.
- They often hold an innate opposition to authority.
- They can find it hard to get on with the full range of personalities in a squad, and can become intolerant of those with less ability.

The challenge for the coach is therefore to integrate the maverick star player into the side, giving them the satisfaction their talents deserve and, more importantly, raising the quality of the team's performances and results.

We can take each of the points listed above in turn.

Difficulty in accepting team goals: This is often because either they are not made fully clear to the player, or he/she has what they believe is a better way. But there are methods to be employed to integrate these players into the goals. Firstly, the star performer could be encouraged to contribute to them – after all, they are the ones who are most likely going to be playing the biggest role in their delivery. Secondly, the maverick will want to know clearly their own role, to stop them trying to play in every position and do everything. So those responsibilities need to be negotiated and explained clearly, then practised in training sessions. Finally, ensure that the maverick (along with the rest of the squad) is fully aware of the big picture those goals are designed to satisfy.

Challenging existing practices: Why not? The ideas of the maverick, just like those of any other player, might lead to improvements in the team. That the maverick challenges usual methodology, alongside our own natural deep lying envy of a more talented individual, means that we can put up a defence to his suggestions. However, the best coaches, just like the best managers in business, health, education, finance and so forth, welcome the ideas of their strongest performers. They are open to suggestions, and prepared to listen to and try out the thoughts of their team. The type of coach who pushes away the maverick star player for offering their views is the kind of coach who is over sensitive, and uncomfortable in their own authority. It is not the maverick who has the problem here… and they are likely to take their talents elsewhere before too long.

Creativity: The star player of this type needs the opportunity to express themselves during matches, and so their role in the team structure must allow for this. At the same time, delegating responsibility during training for solving team problems will bring the best out of the maverick, and help him integrate with his fellow players.

Questioning: The good coach will recognise that the questions of the maverick star player might not be put over in the best way, but will respond positively and honestly, and in a non-judgemental way. When this player feels he has been given a cold shoulder to his legitimate question, respect will be lost, and along with this, his support.

Opposition to Authority: The coach should carry the responsibility for making the ultimate decision. Players need to respect this, but the star player does need the respect of given the opportunity to offer their input, along with senior players and, at times, newer members of the squad. If the star player sees the unit as a team, with the coach playing a different, but nonetheless important role for the collective good, then the authority they hold is deserved, rather than simply expected, then he is likely to be more supportive.

Getting on with team mates: If the star player, or any other team member for that matter, does not get on with their team mates this is only a problem if it is allowed to become one. Teams in many parts of life are not necessarily made up of friends, but simply of people who can work together effectively. It is the coach's man management skills that can create the environment for this to occur.

What we can therefore conclude is that a successful coach will integrate their star player into the team. But many of the ways to do this, as outlined above, are ones which can and should be applied to all team members to get the best out of the side. In the end, it comes down to man management skills, and finding the most effective ways to get the most out of every single player in achieving the goals of the team.

However, ultimately, no one person is bigger than the team. That includes the coach. It also includes single players, even if they are the best you have.

Individual Passing Drills

General Information on Diagrams

Most of the drills described over the next chapters include a simple explanatory diagram. For these, the dots represent players and the lines refer to the movement of the ball (white) and movement of players (black). Sometimes, a square is used to show the need for grid (painted, or made of cones) and lines are added to divide up areas of the pitch. A small grey circle represents the ball. Wherever possible, the white 'players' represent the side in possession and the black (plus occasionally grey) represent the opposition.

Another point to keep in mind, especially if you look to adapt these drills to your own team's particular needs, or to address your own requirements as a player, is that once they become too complicated, they lose their effectiveness. The object of the drills is to practise a particular technique, keep that objective at the forefront of your thinking.

Drill One – The Lay Off

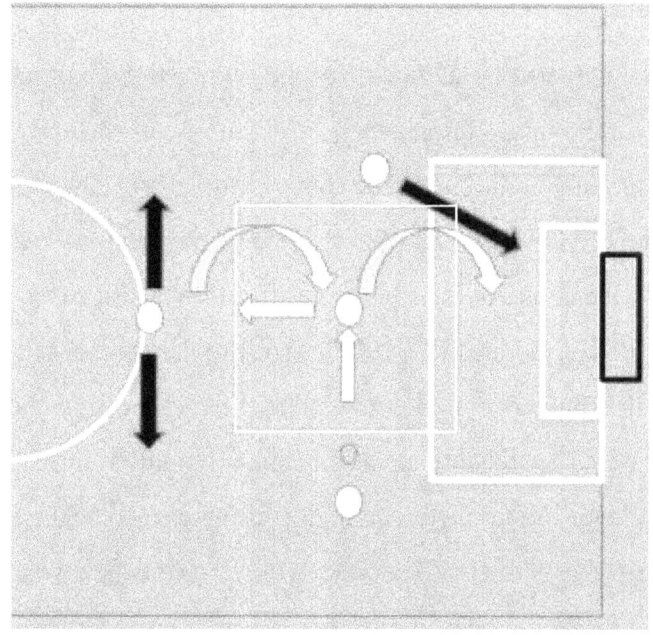

This drill is one that will help individual players gain a rapid and effective control of the ball. It will then assist them to pass with the first or second touch to inject speed into an attack, protect the ball or make a counter attack (an attack on the break) with pace and precision.

Four attacking players make use of a grid or square, about 12 x 12 meters. This can be set up with cones, or marked on your training area. Indeed, a series of such grids, for example 3 x 2, makes an excellent resource for number of drills.

The four attacking players line up with one on each of three sides of the grid, and the fourth in the centre of the grid. Remember, the objective is to control the ball and lay it off with one or two touches maximum.

The players on the outside of the grid feed the ball into the player in the centre – this is the player who is gaining most from the drill. (For this reason, positions should be rotated regularly). The ball can be fed in to feet, off the ground, to the thigh, the chest and the head. The player in the centre adjusts his feet to get into position to control the ball correctly, and lays it off (either back to the feeder, and often to one of the other players) – sometimes with the first touch, sometimes with the second. The 'feeders' should be mobile on their line, to all the central player to find different angles for his lay off. Sometimes the feeder can throw the ball for either a cushioned header or a flick on. With the flick on, one of the 'spare' feeders makes a run to the unused side of the square to take possession.

The key skills to look out for are:

- Body position receiving the ball – encourage the half turn with shoulder angled towards the feeder.
- Arms out for balance.
- Cushioning the ball on control
- A firm lay off.
- Speed in the drill, it should be a fast-paced practice.

Development

By adding in a defender to put pressure on the receiver, the practice becomes more realistic to the game situation.

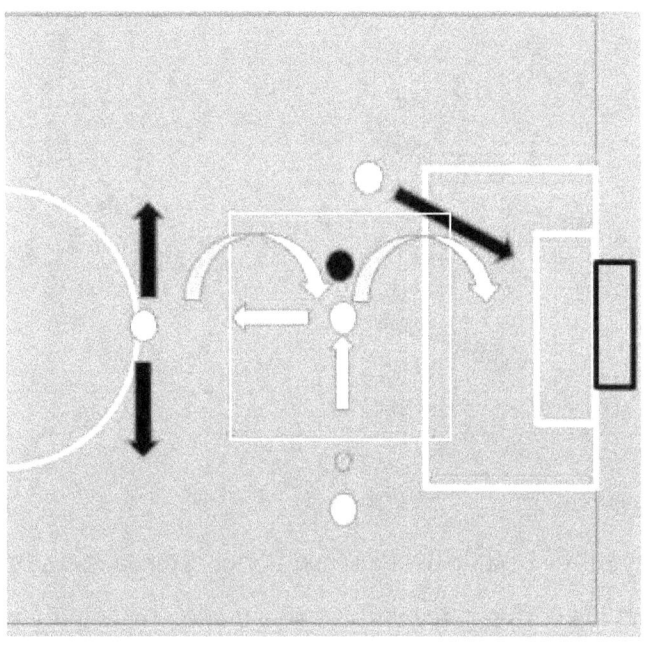

Drill Two: Pass and Shoot

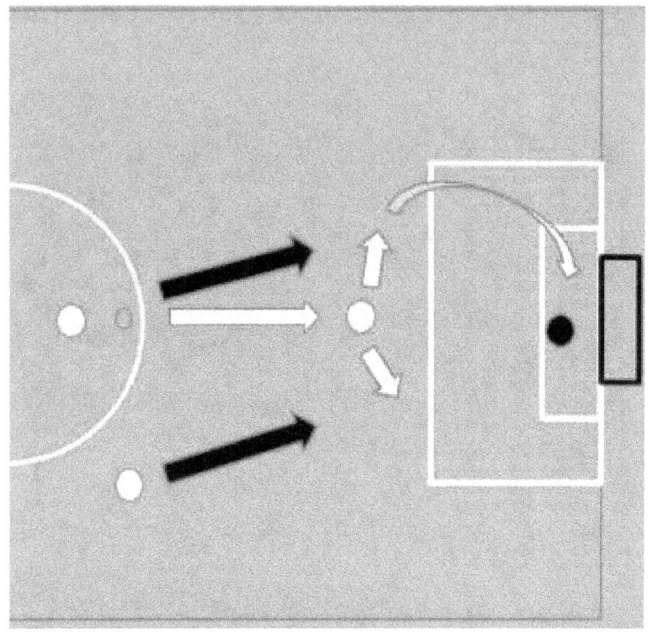

Like many of the best drills, Pass and Shoot offers a focus on the skill in hand, but also offers a realistic game situation by helping to develop other important techniques. It features, in its basic form, four players – three offensive players and a goalkeeper. One play is located on the edge of the D of the penalty area. The ball is fed in to this player by another approximately 10 to 15 meters away. This feeder runs on from his pass for a lay off. A third attacking player makes a run towards the penalty area to the other side of central receiver. This central player on the edge of the D lays off the ball with a short pass to one of the approaching team mates, who shoots first time or after one touch.

The ball should be fed in to feet initially, but as the skill levels improve the ball can be fed in at different levels. Younger players will quickly see that lifting the ball makes it more difficult for the central receiver to lay off the ball accurately, encouraging them to keep it at ground level.

The key skills to look out for are:

- Accurate ball played in to receiver, followed by an immediate run.
- Communication from the two runners as to where they want the ball played
- The receiver playing a cushioned pass so the on-running strikers can hit the ball first time if possible, but definitely after one touch.
- Body position of the receiver, either with back to goal, or on the half turn. Both positions should be practised.

Development

There are many ways to develop this drill. Firstly, in the example below, the receiver lays the ball off wide, for the on-running winger. The winger crosses for the two attackers that are now in the penalty area.

Once this is mastered, the development can go even further. The initial passer runs first to the far post then accelerates into the near post. The initial receiver turns and runs for the far post. Here, the winger is looking to get to the by line to cross, in order to give his team mates time to get into position.

Pulling the ball back from the by line is an effective attacking ploy.

Further development can see the addition of defenders. Firstly, one to put pressure on the receiver, to ensure that his or her control is good, and body position protects the ball. Then a second defender can be added to track the runners.

Although the addition of defenders does turn the drill into more of a team activity than an individual one, specific passing techniques (pass into feet, lay off and cross) are still being developed.

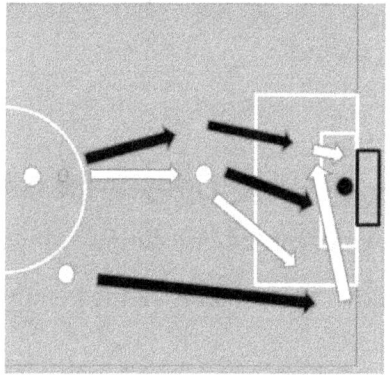

Drill Three – Wall Pass

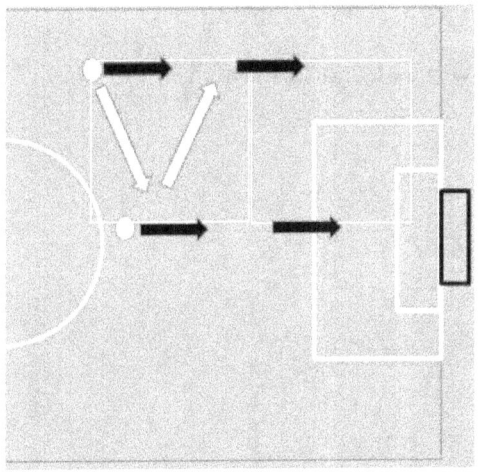

This drill exemplifies the value of simplicity. It involves two players, and is best played using grids, but these are not absolutely necessary. The first stage is for players to pass across the grid diagonally, the team mate moves onto the ball, takes a touch, then passes back. The drill can rapidly move on to players using different pass and control techniques, for example, one player lifts a pass, his team mate controls then lays it back along the ground.

Another way to make the drill tougher is to make the passing first time. This requires greater concentration from the players as they must ensure that they are in the correct position to receive the ball.

The key skills to look out for are:

- Moving the feet to get into position quickly.
- Both players constantly moving forwards.

- Increasing speed in the passing and movements.
- Body position correct for receiving the ball.
- Cushioning the ball with a strong first touch.

Development

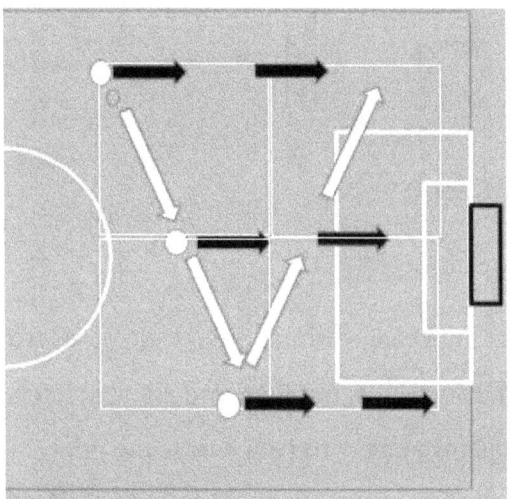

This drill can be developed by the addition of a third player. Now the central player must receive the ball on the half turn, rotate and pass the ball on. The addition of some controlled defence in the middle of the grids (therefore, another two players) will ensure that the passers are accurate and thinking about their delivery, since they will need to make an angle for their passes. The passers can also look to bend the pass by using the outside of the foot, or by lifting the ball slightly.

Whether defence is used or not, one of the key elements of this drill is that the technique of receiving the ball, cushioning it on arrival to ensure that the first touch makes the next pass easy. The development of this needs to take priority over speed, or the defender winning the ball. Therefore, any defensive players will need to play under limitations.

Drill Four – Triangles

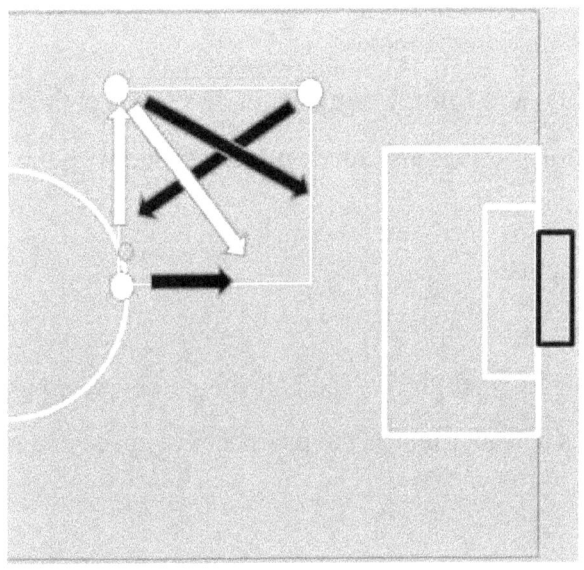

The basis of keeping possession in football is making triangles. Using this method, along with plenty of movement from team mates, will create spaces further forward for more dangerous and incisive passing. This means that there are always two simple passes on for the player in possession of the ball. To ensure that this is the case, players need to be on the move, checking for opposition markers. In this unpressured drill, players should practise mostly playing the ball on the ground, but also lifted passes. Once the ball is off the ground, control is more difficult, and players therefore need to make the triangle smaller in case possession is lost.

Once the basics have been mastered, then the introduction of one defender makes the practice more realistic to the game situation.

The key skills to look out for are:

- Players constantly on the move.
- Precise passing, and control using the body to protect the ball.
- Communication – this is also made more realistic with the addition of a defender.
- Cushioning the ball.
- Firm passing.
- Ball to feet, or lifted slightly. The ball should never be passed in a way that requires a header unless the players have space and are technically strong.

Development

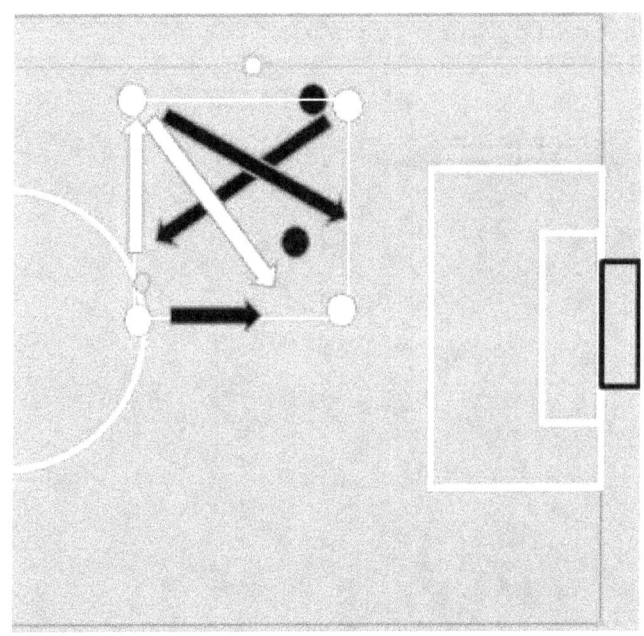

This drill comes to life with the addition of an extra attacker and two defenders. It may be necessary to make the playing area wider, unless the players are particularly strong technically, but the principal of the developed drill remains the same.

Not that the defenders are given very specific roles – the objective of the drill is, after all, to practise passing in triangles, not to win the ball. One defender has responsibility for marking a player (they will need to switch the player marked, as otherwise the drill remains 3 v 1 rather than 4 v 2). The other defender aims to close down the ball.

Movement from the attacking players is essential for the drill to be effective, and they must communicate as they will have little time to find space.

Drill Five – The Pass To Switch Play

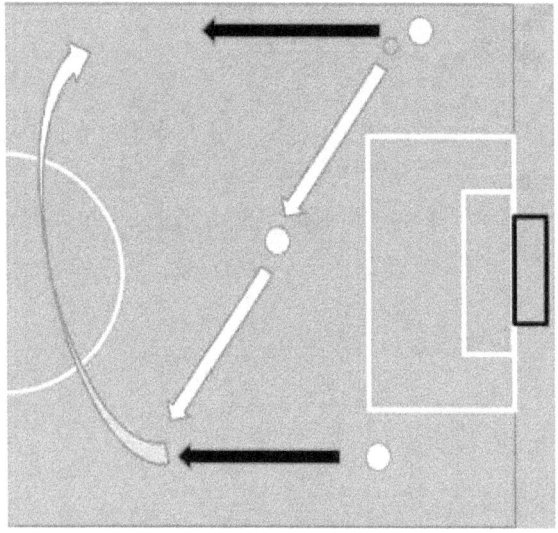

Switching play is an excellent way of creating space further up the pitch, as the opposition's defensive unit must all move to adjust to the new position of the ball. It is also an effective long-term strategy for ensuring that the opposition does more running, and is therefore more tired by the end of the game.

The drill here involves three players (although, an attacking goalkeeper can be added, who starts with the ball and distributes it to one of the full backs). The ball is passed through the central player to the opposite wing. Passing needs to be firm and accurate, and passes need to be quickly brought under control.

Although in a match situation, passers are often under little or no pressure, nevertheless the quicker the ball is switched, the more the challenge for the opposition to re-position their defence.

The final part of the drill is a long cross field ball. This should be lifted for speed, and is a riskier (although quicker) way of switching play, since a long pass is easier to intercept, and harder to play accurately.

The key skills to look out for are:

- Crisp passing.

- Body position for receiving the ball. The central player should be on the half turn. The player receiving the long cross-field ball should be chest on to the pass, as it is likely the pass will arrive above ground.

- Good technique in the long pass; hitting with the laces (an instep pass over this distance is too slow, and is likely to be intercepted) and leaning back slightly to achieve height in the pass.

Development

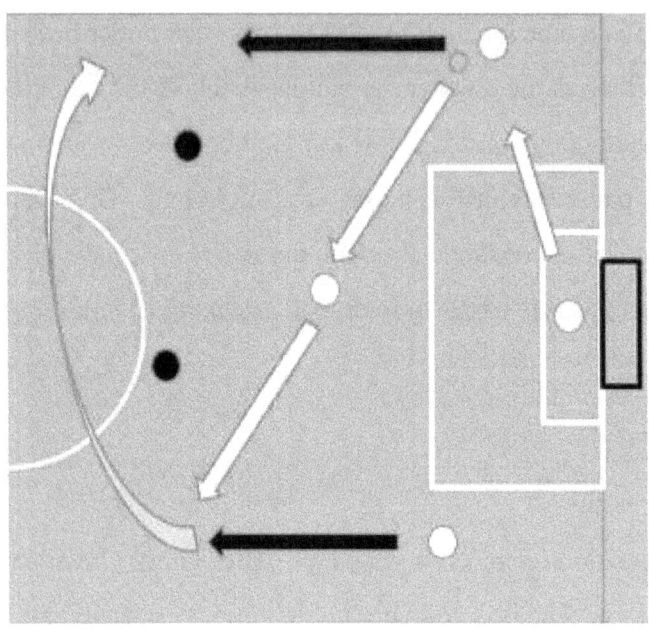

An effective development for this drill is as follows. Introduce (if you have not used one) a goalkeeper and two opposition defenders. The aim for the side in possession is to cross the half way line with the ball under control. It is permissible to use the goalkeeper with a back pass if necessary. By switching play, the attacking side will eventually wear down the defensive players and create the space they need to achieve their objective. In many ways, this drill is an extension of the 'Triangles' activity of the last drill, but is situated in a more realistic match situation.

Again, although this becomes in some ways a team drill, the individual techniques of individual types of passing, good control and communication are still practised and improved.

Team Passing Drills

Drill One: Crossing

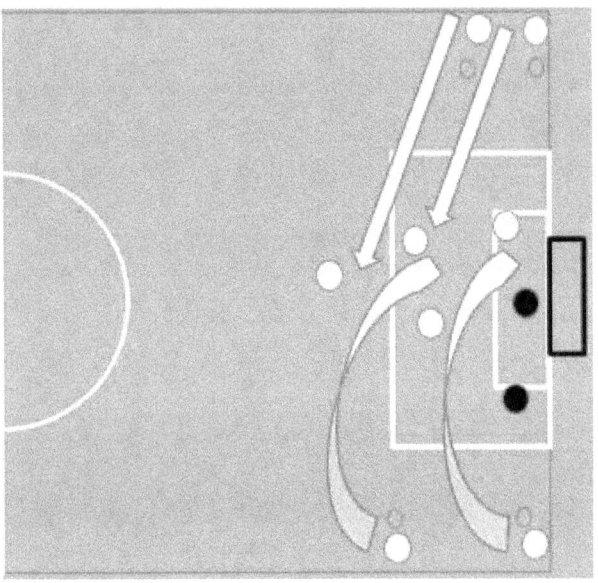

The ability to cross the ball, either in the air or along the ground, adds an extra dimension to both a team's qualities and those of the individual player. Crosses are great levelers – when there is a gulf in class between teams a ball floated in from wide, or driven across the goal causes problems in any defense.

The drill above shows crosses from various positions. The drill can easily be extended to offer dead ball crossing from free kicks as well as corners, and can include both crossing on the move and from a dead ball.

Players should work on both feet, and on hitting dead balls as well as moving balls. They should practice in swingers (left foot from right hand side and right foot from left hand side of the pitch) and also out swingers (opposite to above.) The first of these is easier for the attacking side, as the ball is heading towards the goal, but also easier to defend as the ball flies into the keeper's region, plus the defense can get bodies in the tight area. An out swinger usually means a harder header, as the ball has to be directed back towards goal. However, often there will be less (although still considerable) pressure on the attacker. An out swinger creates a decision for the keeper, as they must decide whether they can get into a clear catching or punching position to clear the danger. If they try and fail, they risk being out of position for the subsequent attempt at a goal.

Numbers are flexible for this drill, but it is advisable to overload attackers as the purpose of the practice is to create goal scoring opportunities. Too many defenders and the chances of an attacker getting on the end of the cross are reduced.

The key skills to look out for are:

- Dead ball – pace and swerve. The ball should be hit with the front of the laces, foot under the ball and with a good follow through to generate power.
- Clearing the near post (as this area will usually be marked by the defence) but not so powerful that the ball travels beyond the attackers.

- Variety, so sometimes pulling the ball back for an arriving midfielder to cross into the box, thus changing the angle of attack.
- Moving ball – Aerial cross; arms for balance and leaning slightly backwards for height; front of the laces hitting low and cleanly on the ball.
- Low, driven cross – good decision making – if the defence is in position then the cross will be cut out if driven across goal.
- Pulling back for players to run on to, taking the goalkeeper out of the equation as they cannot reach the ball.
- Usually near post, as this gives the keeper less chance and means that the defence has less time to organise. Driven hard, an own goal is a regular result as defenders struggle to get their body position in line to clear.

Development

There are many ways to develop the drill. Starting with the ball deeper and passing wide creates a situation whereby the defence has less time to be organised. Setting a clear offside line (normally, in the game situation, there would be more defenders and possible less attackers if the cross comes from open play) adds realism.

The drill can also be adapted for straight shots at goal from free kicks. Here, the ball should be placed in different positions to change the attack. Most teams will have one or two dead ball specialists who will take free kicks in range for a shot, and perhaps corners.

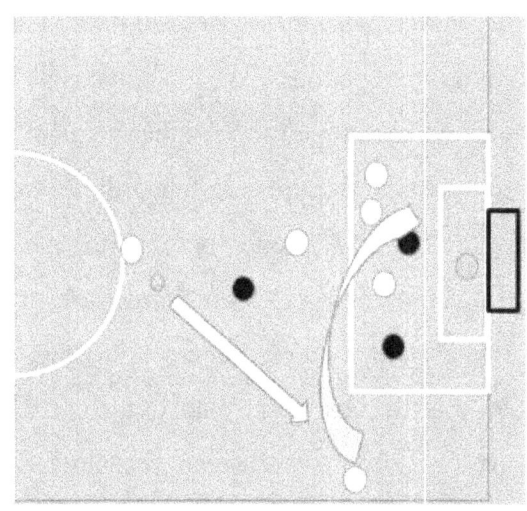

Drill Two: Retaining Possession and Passing Forwards

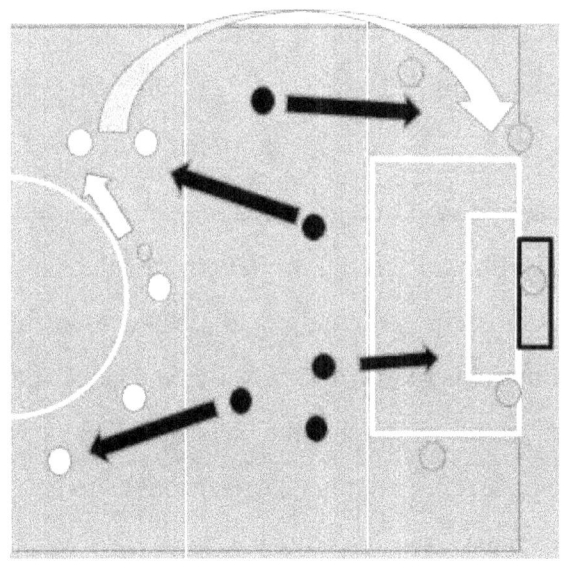

This is one of my favorite drills because it addresses so many soccer issues. The teams are divided into three groups of five or six, and half a pitch is divided into three sections. The objective is as follows: to pass the ball from one end sector to the other. However, players from the middle section try to stop this. In this drill, up to two players are allowed to leave the central section to pressure the ball and stop the pass to the other end being made. The remaining three or four players (black, in the diagram above) attempt to intercept the pass. If they are unsuccessful, it becomes the task of the team at the other end (grey, above) to make the pass back to the white team. Again, two members of the black side move to pressure the ball as soon as it enters the greys' zone.

If the ball goes out of play, is intercepted or the pass across is unsuccessful, the team in the middle swap with the team who failed to make the cross.

Short and long passing skills are practiced in a semi pressured environment, communication is essential, from both the attacking and defending units. Decision making is required, to pick the moment to make the long pass. Control is required, especially on receipt of the long pass as the central team can pressure the ball as soon as the ball enters the end zone, and players need to make decisions as to how they can best support the team mate receiving the ball.

The key skills to look out for are:

- Short passing along the ground.
- One or maximum two touches to control and pass.
- Team mates getting into position to support.
- Communication from both attack and defence, with best decisions being made (if you are the coach, be prepared to stop the session regularly to point out good and weak practice).
- A variety of passing, short, long, lifted and along the ground.

Development

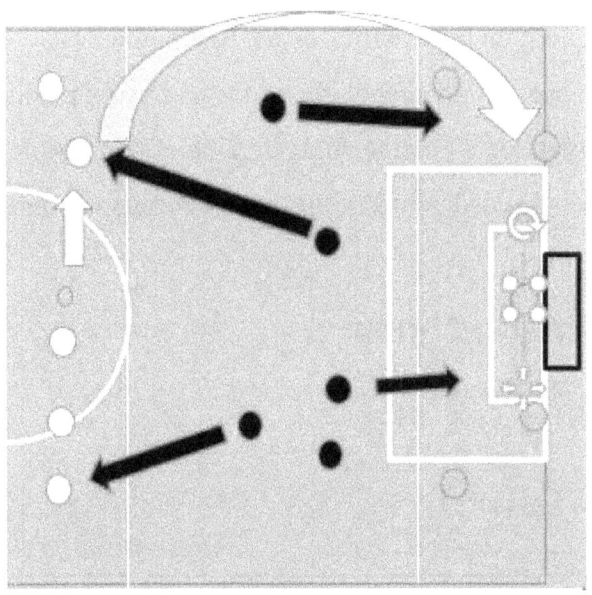

There are many ways to develop the practice. Extending the size of the central area and reducing the area of the end sections puts more pressure on controlling the ball, and means that passing, both short and long, needs to be tight. There is no room for miss-control. Time pressure can be added to help practice, for example, playing the ball out quickly on transition. For example, the long can be required within four touches in total, or within five seconds of receipt of the ball. Equally, teams can practise taking the pace out of the game with a series of passes. To embed this, only one defender is allowed into the end zone, and, for example, there can be a requirement that all players touch the ball in that team.

The best way to develop this excellent drill is to play it, and identify areas of weakness in team and individual skills. The drill can then be adapted to work on those deficiencies. It is a good recommendation to use this drill regularly, in most or every practice session. The quality of team passing, and retention of possession will increase, as well the as added bonus of the team working on pressuring the ball.

Drill Three: Passing Out of Defense

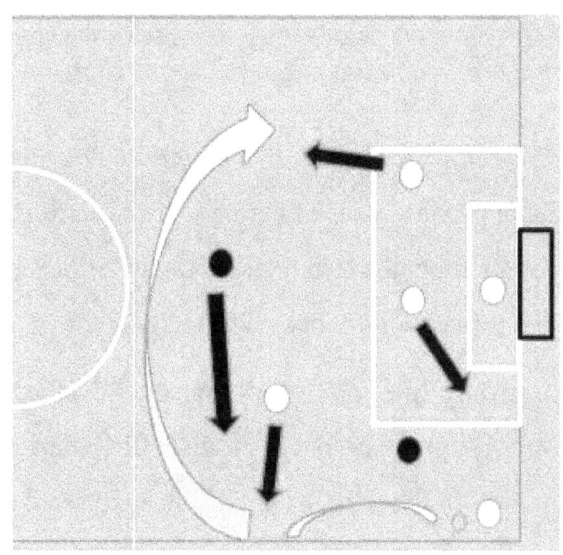

A very important team skill for any side, the ability to pass out of defense means that the ball enters the opponent's half under control. Certainly, there are times when it is just necessary to clear the ball, but generally a side that can build an attack from the back is likely to be more successful. Please note, this drill is not suitable for building an attack on the break, which is a different scenario requiring speed from players and a rapid transfer of the ball forwards.

In the situation on which we are working here, the ball is played with control, creating spare players who can receive the ball without too much pressure. A back pass to the goalkeeper is an option from which the move can begin once more if something goes wrong.

The drill involves five attacking players (whites) including one goalkeeper. Two defenders – in the match situation these will be strikers and midfielders on most occasions – try to close down space and intercept the ball.

The drill begins from either touchline, in a defensive position somewhere in line with the penalty area. One player makes a run towards the touchline for a long ball down the line. Another player comes short to the man in possession to make a triangle.

The ball is lifted down the line and then switched across the pitch, either via a central player or, if there is space, a long ball. Patience is the key, and if control is lost, or the pressuring players are effective in closing space, then the ball is laid back to begin the process once more.

The objective is to get the ball over the half-way line under good control.

The key skills to look out for are:

- A good first touch
- Continued movement from the team to create space
- The ability to play accurate lifted passes and short balls on the ground
- Confidence. Difficult to assess this, but we are looking for players happy to take an extra touch and play the ball backwards if necessary. It is about creating confidence among the defensive players that they are good enough to do more than just hit a long, aimless ball forwards, most probably giving away possession.

Development

This drill can be developed with the addition of an extra defensive player to create a situation where there is additional pressing of the ball. Here, the spare man and the goalkeeper become even more important. The aim is to play shorter passes to reduce the chances of an interception, creating an overlap from the opposite full back to cross the half way line with the ball under control.

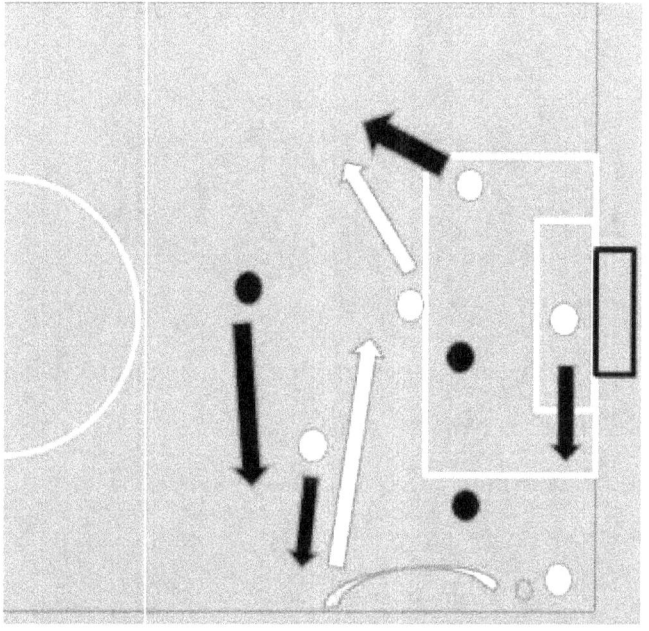

Regular practice of these drills will enable players to develop the confidence to play the ball and make decisions to launch their attacks with the ball successfully controlled out of defence.

Drill Four: Creating Shooting Opportunities

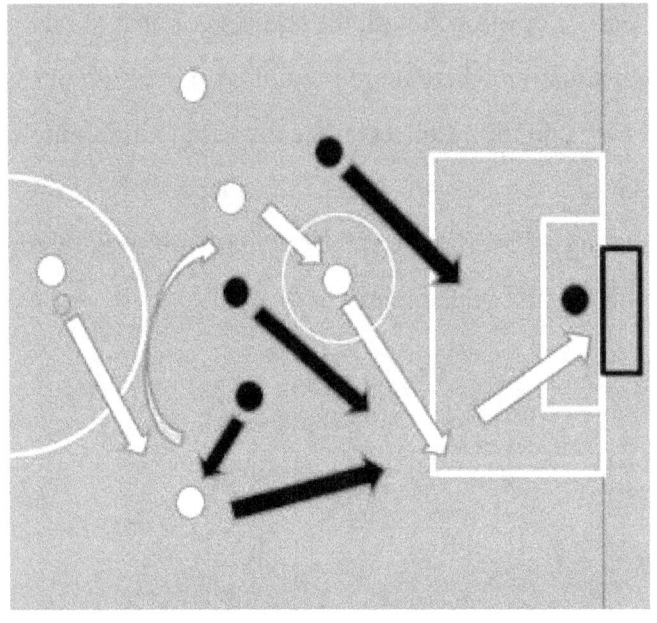

This drill is actually easier than it looks. The key is the player in the circle. This player has a two meter 'protection zone' into which defenders cannot enter. Beyond this, there are five attackers (including the protected one) against three defenders and a keeper. The aim is to create space for a shot on goal through effective running off the ball.

In the example above (the drill can be varied to get other players into shooting positions), the ball is played wide drawing the defense, then switched infield. The wide player making this pass continues his or her run into the box. The ball is fed into the player in the circle, who lays it off to the player making the run. This player shoots.

In the early stages, especially for less experienced players, at the point the protected player makes his pass, the opposition must stop (keeper apart). This enables practice of the objective, i.e. getting a shot on goal.

As the players become more skilled in the drill, defensive movement can be brought back into play.

The key skills to look out for are:

- Movement off the ball.
- Quick one or two touch passing. Pace has to be injected into the move to outplay the defenders.
- The protected player receiving the ball on the half turn.

Development

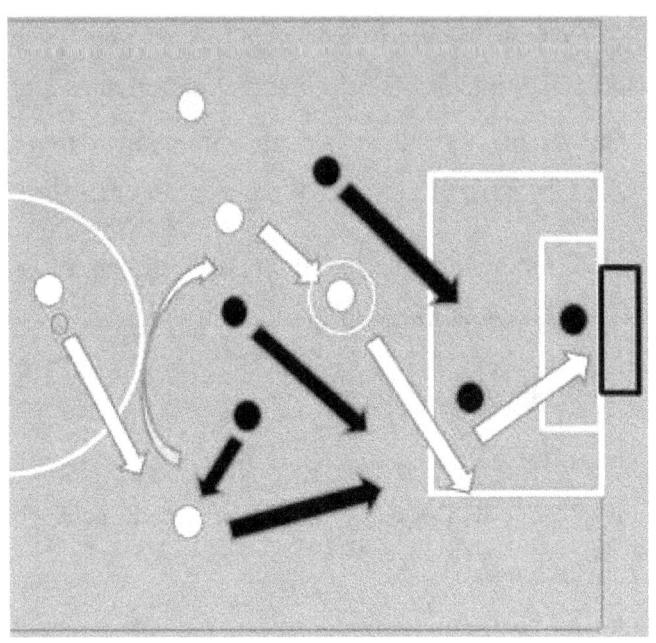

An additional defender, reducing the size of the protected zone and allowing full movement from the defensive players are all ways to develop the drill, making it closer to a real life situation.

Drill Five: Match Play

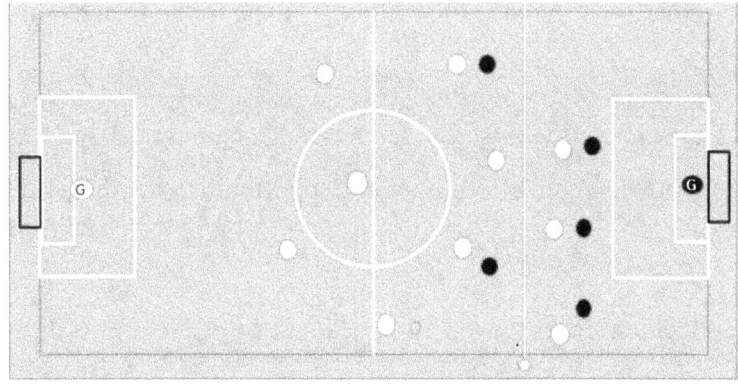

Once basic techniques have been mastered, it is useful to try them in the match situation. However, the match situation should be controlled to allow development of the skills needed to achieve the objective of the drill. In this case, this objective is to create goal scoring opportunities.

In this drill a full team play five defenders and a keeper. The attacking half of the pitch is divided into two. Restrictions apply as follows:

• No defending players in the attacker's half. This means that the whites (attackers) always have the opportunity to start their move again by playing the ball back into their half. This encourages patience and keeps possession.

• The area between the half way line and the 'artificial' line allows only two defenders.

• The area to the goal allows only three defenders.

- The coach may wish to apply limits to the number of attackers allowed in this zone to make the drill as realistic to the match situation as possible.

The attacking side employ the passing techniques – lay off, cross, switch etc. they have practiced creating opportunities for shots on goal.

The key skills to look out for are:

- Judgement from the attacking team as to when to pass into the final quarter. It is worth the coach stopping the game from time to time to point out good play and where better decisions could be made.
- Ensuring triangles are created.
- Ensuring control is good, with encouragement to receive the ball on the half turn.
- Ball kept on the ground – there is space to do so.
- Individual's technique in control and passing.

Development

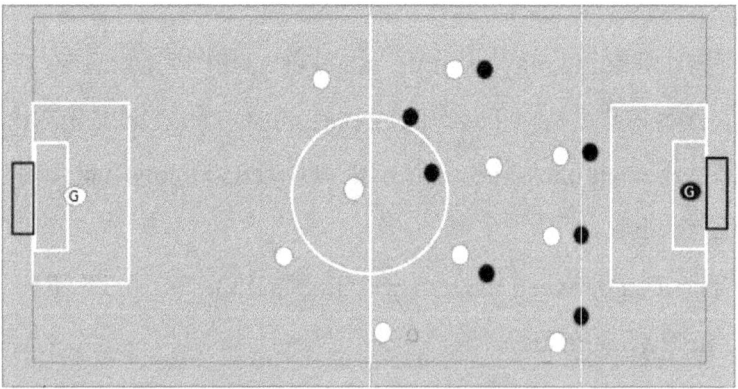

Adding extra defenders, and increasing the areas into which they can move all add further pressure to the attacking side, making the game closer to a real match situation.

Individual Possession Drills

Drill One: Chaos

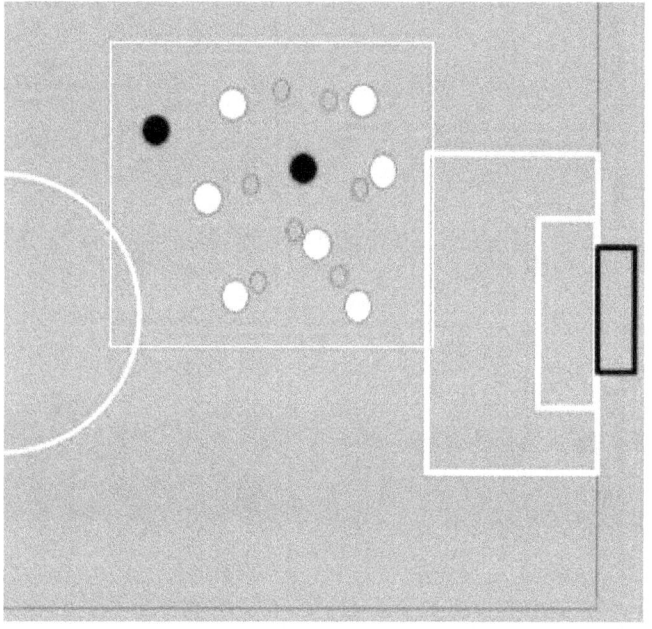

This is an excellent warm up drill, encouraging players to keep the ball. Set up a large grid, perhaps 15m x 15m (or use a penalty area). The number of players involved in flexible, but six or seven players in possession against two opponents works well.

The aim is for the opponents to kick the balls out of the grid, while the players in possession attempt to keep hold of their ball. Once they have lost it out of the grid, they become defenders, trying to dispossess the remaining players. Players in possession must be moving all of the time.

The key skills to look out for are:

- Using the body to protect the ball. Ensure that the body is between the ball and the opponent, playing sideways to the tackler to establish as much distance as possible.
- Employment of individual skills to keep possession, such as step overs, Cruyff turns etc.
- Spotting spaces to dribble into – players should identify spaces away from their tacklers and dribble into it.
- Head up when dribbling – with so many players in a short space, players need to develop spatial awareness.

Development

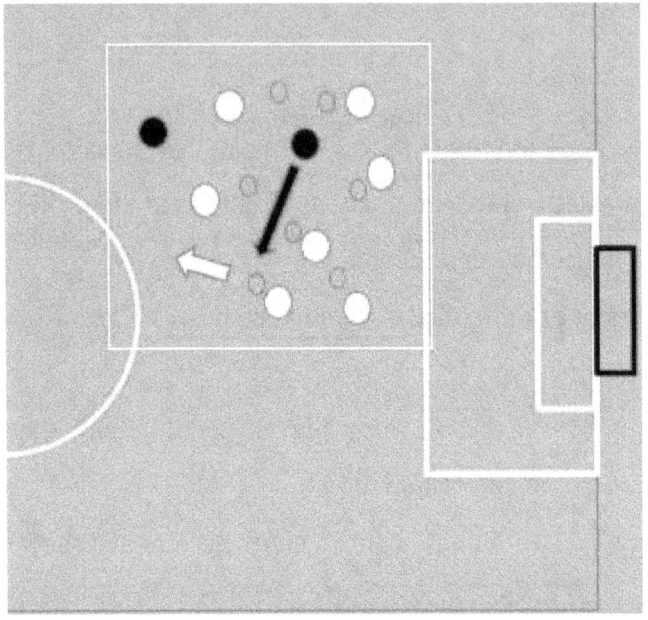

There are several ways to develop the game; shrinking the grid or adding more players leads to extra pressure needing tighter control to retain possession.

An interesting way (shown above) to develop the drill is to allow tacklers to win possession of the ball, rather than just kicking it out of the grid.

Drill Two: 1 v 1

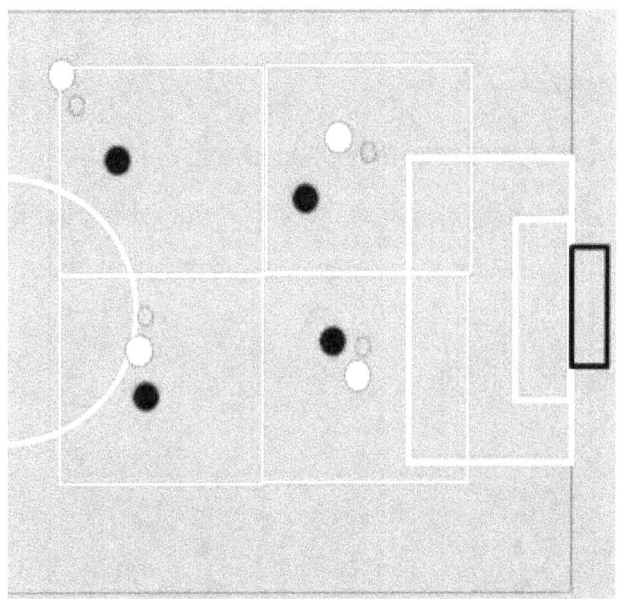

This is a tiring drill, but one that will lead to rapid development of possession skills. Grids are shrunk in size to 5m x 5m. In the grid is a 1 v 1 match where the objective is to keep possession. The white player attempts to hold on to the ball while the opponent (black circle) attempts to win possession.

With younger players, a points system can be used which will maintain interest and encourage the tackler to do more than just kick the ball out of play. If the ball leaves the grid, possession changes and one point is awarded to the tackler. However, if possession changes hands, three points is awarded. There is an added bonus to this system. Inevitably, disagreement will occur when the ball is not clearly under the control of either player. In this situation, encourage the players themselves to work out what constitutes retaining possession.

The key skills to look out for are:

- Keeping the body between the opponent and the ball.
- Using individual skills, such as the stepover, or dropping the shoulder and moving the other way, to beat an opponent and keep possession.
- Ensure the tackler adheres to the laws of the game.

Development

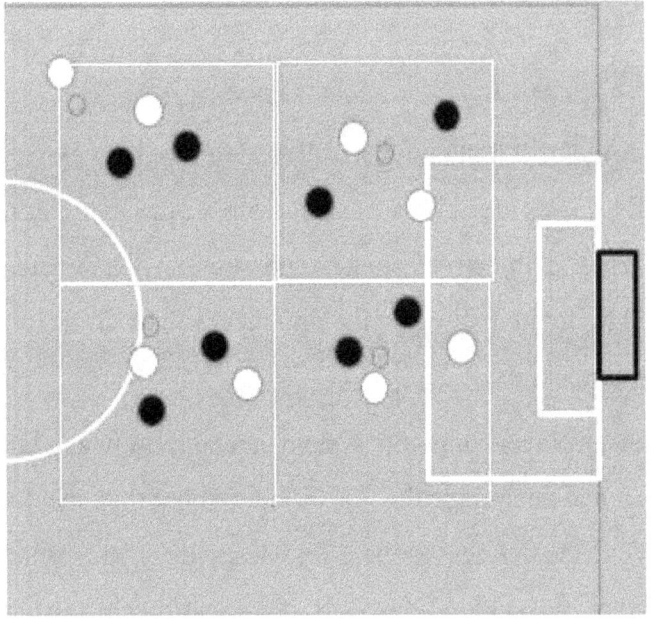

Turning the drill into a 2 v 2 contest changes the dynamics, and adds additional interest by bringing into play passing. Players should have fairly quickly learned to keep the ball 1 v 1, but it is harder against two opponents. Now they will need to communicate, find space and learn to be available for the pass.

Drill Three: Chase

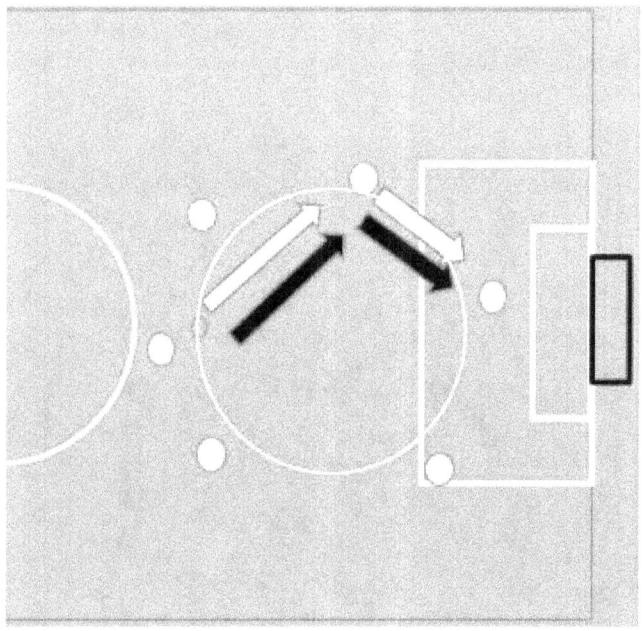

This is a fun possession drill which focusses on keeping the ball through passing rather than close control. Six players are on the outside of large circle. The first player passes the ball to another on the outside of the circle. He or she then follows the ball and tries to win it back. The receiver controls the ball and lays it off to another team mate, then chases that pass.

The key skills to look out for are:

- Good first touch.
- Players on their toes to receive the pass.
- More able players should look to disguise the pass, by dropping their shoulder, or using their eyes to deceive the on-rushing challenger.

Development

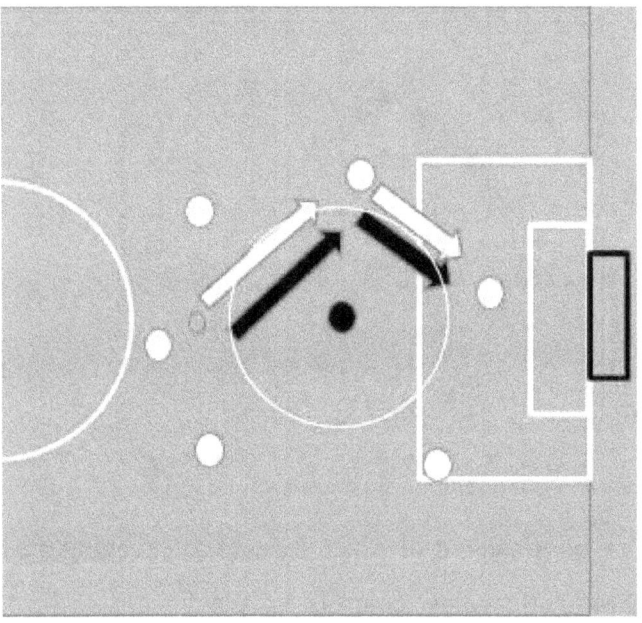

This drill can be made harder by reducing the size of the circle. This means that the first touch of the receiver will need to be perfect. In addition, a defender can be added whose job is to intercept the pass. This reduces the options for the passer, and encourages receivers to become more mobile.

Drill Four: Grid Possession

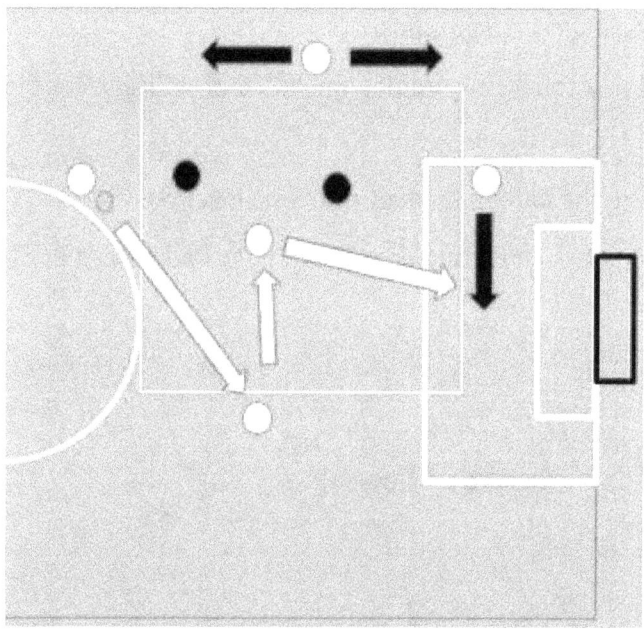

A drill that offers a variation based on a number of grid based exercises. Here, the objective is to retain possession – a target of twenty passes is a good one to set. There are five attackers, one on each side of the 10 x 10 metre grid, plus one inside the grid.

There are two defenders.

The aim is to keep possession by passing, either a short pass into the center, or round the outside of the grid. Encourage the players to move to split the defenders, so that an easy pass is always on. This is a fast-paced activity, with players shifting their body and the ball to create the space for the pass.

The key skills to look out for are:

- Firm passing on the ground.
- A good first touch, cushioning the ball and setting it for the next pass.
- Receiving the ball on the half turn whenever possible.
- Central player, in particular, receiving the ball so that her body is protecting it.

Development

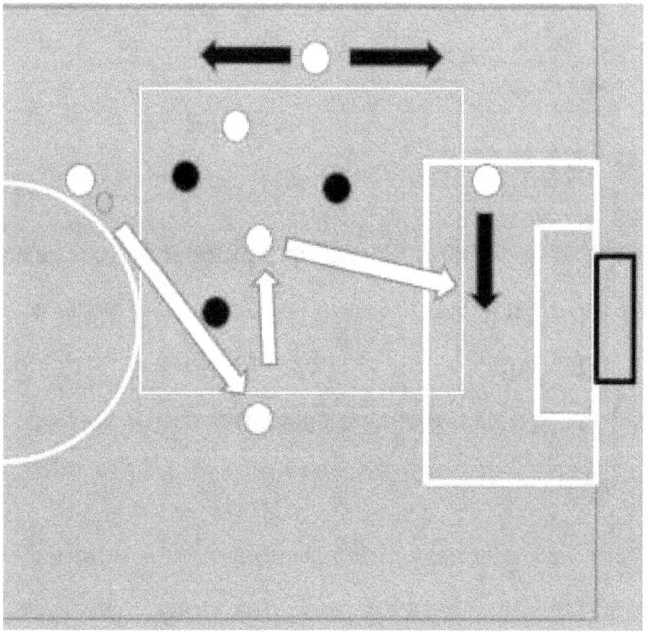

Adding an extra defender and extra attacker inside the grid makes it a more challenging activity. The principles needed to retain possession are unchanged, but there is less time and space inside the grid.

Drill Five: Individual Skills

At some point during a session, often at the beginning, or perhaps when there is a focus on a specific part of the team, and others need an activity to keep them working, a skills circuit is a good idea.

Give the players their own ball, as this is very much an individual activity. Set up cones for dribbling, with another set spaced further apart to work on running into space. Have an area for juggling, a goal for dribbling one on one with a keeper and any other activities appropriate for addressing specific needs of players.

This session can be ended with a group juggling session, for example keeping the ball off the ground through volleys, heading, chesting etc to team mates. Set a target of ten juggles per team, especially with younger groups where a challenge provides great motivation.

Team Possession Drills

Drill One: Short and Long Pass to Create Space

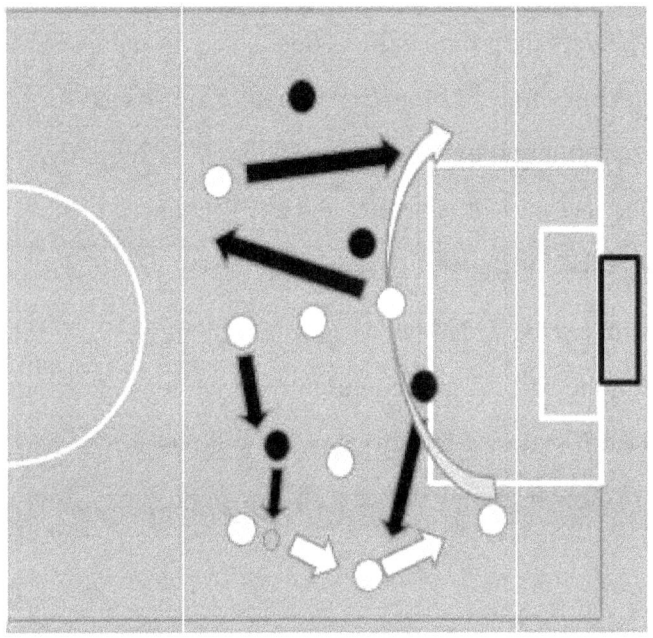

This drill aims to help a team create space by playing a series of short passes to draw the defense out of position, creating space for the long pass into space for a player to run on to. It is an 8 v 4 game, played in a large area, for example a quarter of a pitch, playing across the field.

As with most drills, touch, precision of pass, decision making, movement and communication are all essential in achieving success.

The key skills to look out for are:

- Short passing that is accurate, and one or two touch.
- Movement off the ball to create space.
- Communication.
- An accurate, lofted pass to move the ball up the pitch.

Development

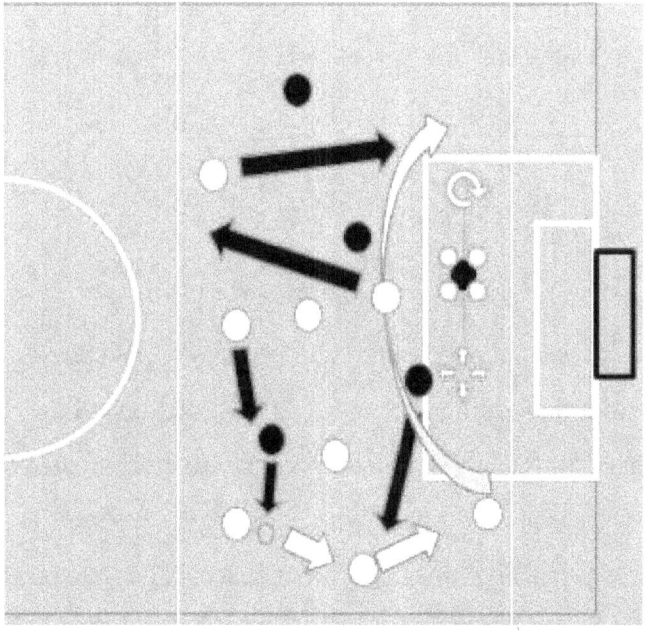

The addition of an extra defender makes the drill more difficult, but still achievable. The pitch area can be shortened, but needs to be big enough to allow for the long pass.

Drill Two: 5 v 2 One or Two Touch

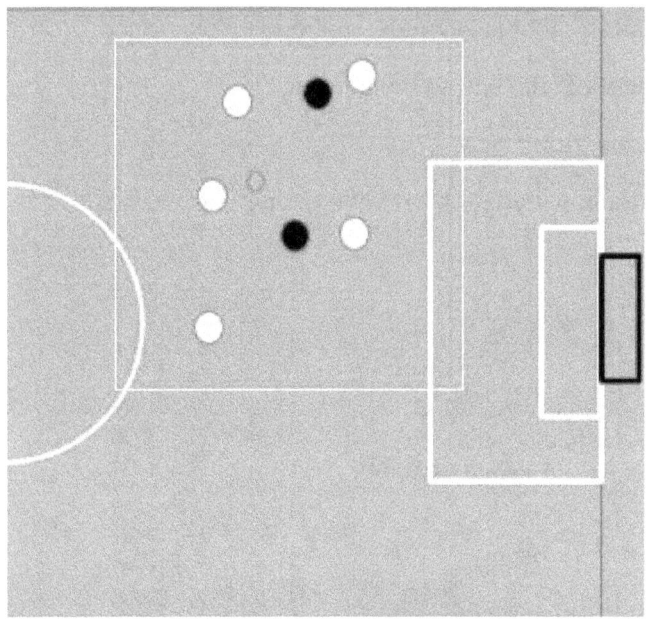

Retaining possession as a team under pressure is, of course, substantially harder than doing it in space. Therefore, one of the objectives of this drill is to move the ball quickly to create that space. The drill employs a 15m x 15m grid with a 5 v 2 game inside. The aim is to keep possession through the creation of space. The space is created with fast, one or two touch passing, a good first touch and lots of movement and communication.

For younger, or less able players, it may be necessary to limit the range of tackling allowed for the defense until confidence and touch is strengthened.

This drill is going well when it is fast, with lots of communication and movement.

The key skills to look out for are:

- Strong first touch, cushioning the ball and positioning it for a quick pass.
- Body position on receiving the ball.
- Communication
- Movement off the ball.

Development

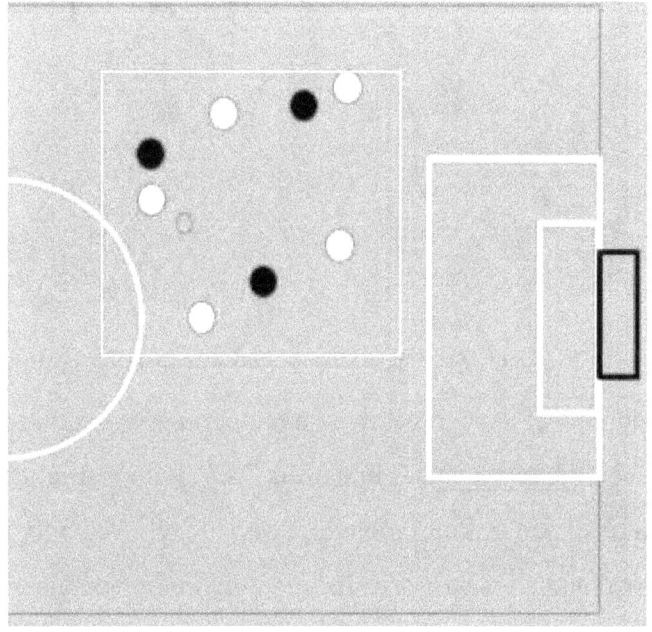

There are various ways to develop this activity. Introducing an extra defender works well, although this player will often need to be prevented from intercepting the pass, as there is insufficient space in the grid to allow this. Another method is to reduce the size of the grid, allow only one touch passing and so forth.

Drill Three: Controlled Game

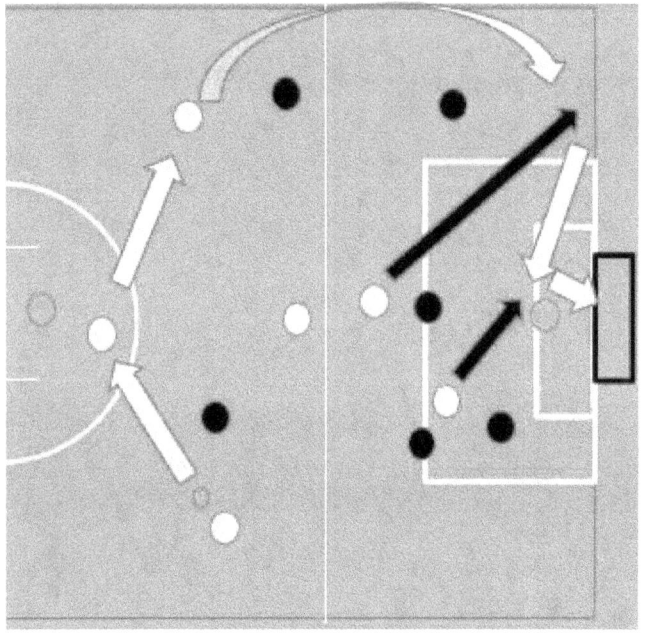

This drill combines short passing to draw in defenders and make space, with injections of pace to get in an attempt on goal. A half pitch has a goal at each end, and a center line. It is 7 v 7, with restrictions. Each side has a goalkeeper; four defenders, who are allowed only in their half, and two attackers who are allowed only in the opponent's half of the pitch.

Short passing creates space for a longer pass. The movement of the attackers creates room for a fast attack. Although players' movements are restricted, the ball can be passed anywhere

The key skills to look out for are:

- Communication.
- Running off the ball.
- These two are essential in this game, as the attackers are heavily outnumbered and will need to attack with pace and precision. The pass into them therefore needs to be of the highest quality.

Development

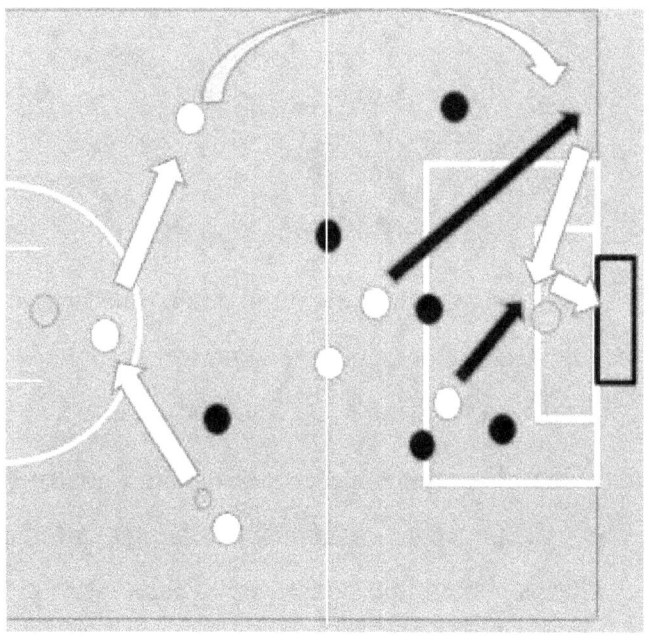

This drill can be developed by allowing one player on each side to play anywhere, and move between zones. This can firstly be a designated player, then the drill can advance to allow any player to move between zones, but with neither team ever having more than five players (plus the keeper) in the defending zone and three in the attacking area. This makes the drill more fluid, and more like a real match situation.

Drill Four: Turncoats

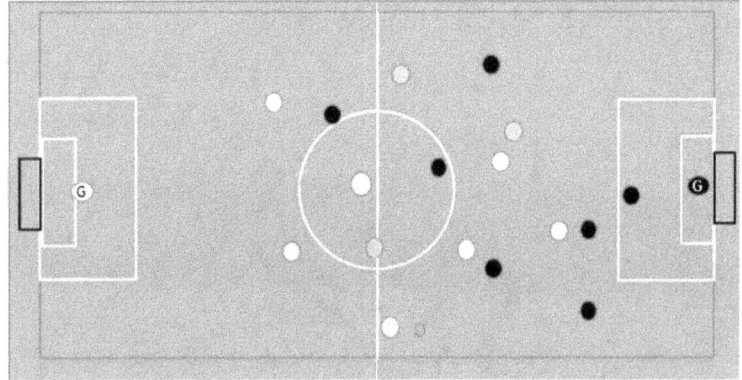

The final two drills involve use of the full pitch. The first, above, is weighted to give the team in possession a numerical advantage, making it easier for them to maintain possession and create space.

Two eight a side team play, with each side having a goalkeeper. Three other players – the turncoats – also play. Wearing a different shirt, or bib, they always play for the side in possession.

Play the game as per a normal match, playing for around twenty minutes to allow the game to develop. (it might be necessary to swap the turncoats, as they will be undertaking more running, playing for both teams.)

The key skills to look out for are:

- *Turncoats:* Finding space during the transition of possession.
- *Others:* Concentrate on the transition phase.
- Check the standard techniques outlined throughout this book.

Development

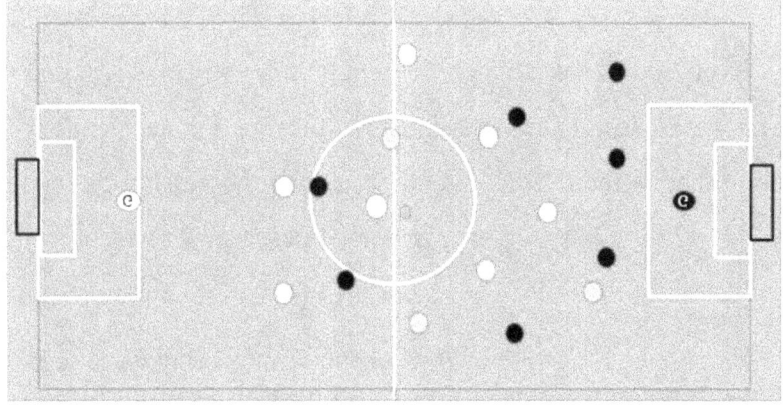

Identify what elements of the players work needs most attention. If control is struggling, perhaps institute a no tackling rule for a spell. If the players find it hard to introduce speed into their attacks, make the game one or two touch. If the players give away possession too readily, introduce a five-pass rule whereby there must be five short passes before the ball is moved far forward at the transition point. Restrict defenders during those five passes.

Drill Five: Match Play

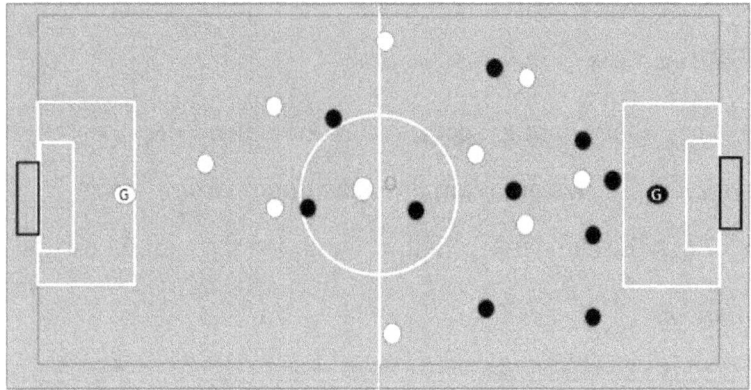

Everybody likes a match! Often, practice sessions will end with a full-on game. But do take advantage of players' enthusiasm for this by offering them a focus. It could be on keeping possession (with younger players, award 'goals' for, say, five good passes in a row), or switching play.

Be prepared to stop matches to point out good play, or to highlight errors or tactical weakness (without picking on individuals.)

Keep the end of session match fun – players are there to enjoy themselves, but do introduce coaching points relevant to the focus of the session the coach has just run.

Conclusion

When we play soccer, we do so for many reasons – it helps us to stay fit and healthy, there is the pleasure that comes from being part of a team, which is where soccer scores over individual sports such as squash or tennis. There is the chance to satisfy the competitive instincts most of us hold, and there is the post-match camaraderie. Soccer gives us a chance to really enjoy ourselves, and it is both the most complex of sports, with high level tactics and technique, but at the same time one that we can play at any level, needing just a ball (and perhaps a couple of jumpers to act as goal posts.

That fun element is crucial; when the game ceases to be a joy, then perhaps it is time to spend our time doing something else. But this absolutely appropriate wish to have fun does not contradict a wish to play the game to as high as standard as we can. For this, we can take our lead from the professional teams, with their (often) highly paid players. We can use the drills and motivations that lead these purveyors of the sport to the top of the soccer tree.

That is a good thing. The drills and practices, the emphasis on team work for passing and possession we have put forward in this book will help us all become better players or more effective coaches.

We have offered here the basic outline of drills. The best coaches and most effective players will now go a step further, adapting the basic drills to the needs of their own team and its component parts. They will devise variations which enable a focus on the particular requirements of their side.

Have great fun coaching, playing and watching the most popular sport in the world.

www.ingramcontent.com/pod-product-compliance
Lightning Source LLC
Chambersburg PA
CBHW072106290426
44110CB00014B/1849